Disclaimer:

Please read the Disclaimer carefully before you read this book. You accept and agree to be bound and abide by the Disclaimer. The information contained on this book is for educational and informational purposes only. The information contained on this book is not intended as, and shall not be understood or construed as, professional advice.

The brand names or logos discussed in this book are property of their respective owners.

Introduction..5
Why a Gym owner requires a marketing consultant
....7
Why gym must appoint you as a marketing
consultant..9
How to approach the gym......................................11
Things to do after the appointment........................13
Handling the project...15
Marketing strategies for your client.......................17
Working with independent contractors..................24

FROM BROKE TO BANK: STEP BY STEP GUIDE TO HOME BASED GYM MARKETING CONSULTING BUSINESS

Soham M.

Copyright © 2018

All rights reserved. No part of this book may be reproduced or transmitted in any form or by any means, electronic or mechanical, including photocopying, recording or by any information storage and retrieval system without written permission of the publisher, except for the inclusion of brief quotations in a review.

Introduction

A business might offer different products or services to customers but their end goal remains the same, which is to procure more customers for expansion and growth. A business requires the help of specialists to help achieve their goals. Big corporations can afford to pay salaries and create a separate department dedicated to marketing functions but for a small business owner, it becomes very difficult to recruit people specifically for marketing. Most of the small business owners take care of marketing functions themselves. It is here that a freelance marketing consultant can help. A marketing consultant can be hired for short duration for specific activity but his expertise will immensely benefit the small business because of the experience and the perspective he brings along with him.

Hiring an external marketing consultant leaves ample time for the owners of small business to focus on their core business. This kind of arrangement ultimately benefits the business. This book focuses on marketing consultancy for local gymnasiums. It provides Insight into various marketing strategies that a local gym can embrace for growth and expansion.

Why a Gym owner requires a marketing consultant

Running and establishing a gym is one thing and establishing an online presence is another. The online world is becoming increasingly competitive, and a business cannot afford to ignore the online community for its growth. Here are a few reasons why a Gym owner might require a marketing consultant.

A business might have created a presence on social media but it is not enough to create a presence. It requires a thorough understanding of social interactions, and a marketing consultant can help with marketing campaigns that are geared to increase the engagement with potential customers. He can help the business to reach a wider audience that was neglected before.

Marketing is all about gaining new clients in a fairly competitive market. An experienced marketing consultant can suggest steps to be taken to encourage customers to buy the membership or other products offered by the gym.

A marketing consultant is a person who has an expertise and also has access to a qualified team of specialist that can accomplish the goal of reaching new customers and converting them as customers for the gym. A gym might have its own website but simply having a website is not enough, it has to be optimized to increase the engagement of the user on the website and also rank higher in search results than its competitors.

A marketing consultant knows the importance of building the brand because the customer feels proud to be associated with certain brands. A marketing consultant can help to increase the brand identity and visibility in the competitive marketplace. By helping the gym to establish its own brand, a consultant can help the gym to distinguish itself from its competitors.

A marketing consultant knows how to transmit the information to the customer. He understands the importance of the communication and can suggest proper communication channels to reach prospective clients thus providing a head start compared to the competitors.

In a cutthroat competitive world, it has become important for businesses to stay closer to their customers, and a marketing consultant can help the business to find ways to connect to the customer. The constant customer interaction can help the business not only to grow but also to gain the trust and confidence of the customer.

By appointing a marketing consultant at Gym owner can focus on managing his gym better. This will lead to increase customer satisfaction which will eventually benefit the gym in the long run.

Why gym must appoint you as a marketing consultant

You have to convince a gym owner about your ability to maximize his return on investment on various marketing campaigns. You can also showcase various projects that have been undertaken by you successfully, in case if this is your first project then you can project confidence and showcase your team of specialists that can design effective marketing campaigns and deliver results.

You have to carry out a small research before approaching the client, this is necessary to demonstrate your commitment to the work. For example, you can research a gym's website. There are various free tools available to analyze the website. With the help of one such tool, you can prepare a small report that highlights the improvements required in the website. For example, if the website is cluttered or has very little information in it then you can suggest ways to simplify the navigational structure or put in more content like pictures or videos that can attract the attention of the customer. You can perform an analysis of the website content and point out the improvements to be done to attract potential customers. This small step can go long way in convincing your prospective client that you mean business and you know your job well.

If the gym owner is hesitant then there could be several reasons and one of them could be that he has some bad experience with some incompetent marketer, or he does not have adequate knowledge about marketing. You have to patiently deal with any kind of resistance offered by him. Your mannerism should convince that you are meeting him to offer better solutions for his business marketing that will benefit him and his business.

How to approach the gym

If you have got any apprehensions of meeting new people then you must practice your sales script adequately. This kind of practice in front of a mirror or a dummy customer can increase your confidence tremendously and make you appear naturally confident in front of the client.

The first step is to identify all the possible objections that the client might have and write them in chronological order. Then prepare sales script, Write down everything that you are going to say, begin a script with the greeting and introducing yourself, make sure to quickly transition a conversation to his business to make him comfortable.

Once you have written your sales script and incorporated all the possible objections from the client, it is time to practice it. You can practice in front of the mirror and carefully watch your expressions or movement of your hands. You must speak in such a way that you don't appear aggressive to the potential customer. The flow of conversation should be natural and very little stress must be put on obtaining the business, rather the focus must be on helping the customer.

You have to be very clear about what you expect from the client and what you are going to deliver in terms of benefit to his business. Such clarity will have a positive impact in the mind of the gym owner. Always remember that marketing is about establishing relationships and your focus must be to establish a good relationship with your potential client and not seek immediate business.

You can ask your friend to act as a dummy customer and rehearse the entire sales script in front of him. If possible you can even ask someone to record your presentation so that you can identify the fault areas in your body language or facial expressions while speaking to the client. These steps will help you to become naturally confident and increase your chances for getting more business from people.

Things to do after the appointment

As soon as you are appointed the marketing consultant for the gym your first steps should be to identify the strengths and weaknesses of the gym. Here you don't have to identify the operational deficiencies. You have to analyze everything from the marketing point of view.

The first job is to visit various gyms in the area and write down the services offered by them and various packages. Make a comparison chart of each service along with the service offered by your client. You can even compare various membership packages offered by your client and other gyms. This will help you to design a better value proposition for your client's gym.

You can even explore if the gym is servicing a different set of customers who have different requirements or is it focused purely on bodybuilding. The segment of customers can be identified for better targeting and positioning of the gym. For example, the gym can introduce weight loss plans for housewives, rehabilitation exercises for people who are suffering from minor damages, special packages for students, etc. All these factors provide the motivation to join the gym.

The next step is to analyze what is to maintain an online presence, for example, you have to deal with the shortcomings in the website and social media. Prepare the list of things to do, for example, if the Facebook page requires an overhaul, like changing the cover, providing the customer with better access to the facilities offered by the gym. You can even set up a system where if the customer posts a query on Facebook then it could be resolved quickly and satisfactorily.

You must also look for any positive or negative reviews that your client has received on the Internet and make note of each review. If the client has not interacted with or responded to such reviews then you can make a note of it to do it at a later stage. If there are negative reviews about your client, a note of them must be made too. In short, everything that could have resulted in interaction with existing or potential customers should be noted and marked for appropriate action.

Handling the project

As a consultant, you are the link between your client and the team that is working on the project. Your team might comprise of a web developer, graphic designer and a copywriter. As a consultant, your job is to monitor every process, right from creating editing the content to monitoring the performance of advertisements created in a PPC campaign. Your marketing strategy should be aligned with the goals of your client. It is your duty as a marketing consultant to formulate a sound strategy to maximize business for your client.

As a marketing consultant, you will be attending and organize the meetings with the client to keep him abreast of the developments, and also attending regular brainstorming sessions with your team to monitor the progress of various campaigns. You will be allocating various tasks to the team members and ensuring that they are completed on time. You are responsible for the smooth functioning of the team at the same time ensuring that the budget does not go overboard and kill the campaign.

You will be required to prepare a weekly report and present it to the client to keep you in the loop. The report could highlight various activities undertaken by you and the results that have been achieved so far.

The report must be prepared with the help of graphs and suitable commentary keeping in mind that your client might not be as tech-savvy as you are. A comparison chart can give a better idea of how things have changed for better after you have taken over as a marketing consultant.

You will also have to track the competitors on the regular basis, you will have to sign up on your website to receive any kind of promotional offers that they might launch to attract existing as well as new customers and inform your clients of such development. You will also be responsible for responding to the queries that are received from the potential customers through the website.

Marketing strategies for your client

You have to come up with innovative marketing solutions to attract new customers for your client's gym.

You can start a referral program for existing members, and encourage the existing members to bring their friends and relatives for free sessions in the gym to experience the services offered by it. The lure of free sessions will attract people to try out the gym and it is here that the gym can capitalize all its strength and services to convert the free session into a paid membership. If someone buys the membership then some form of a rebate or cash incentive could be given to the referring member as a token of appreciation. This small gesture will encourage the people to spread a word about the gym.

You can even encourage the existing members of the gym to post the photographs of their workouts in their social media accounts and for doing so you can reward them with renewal discounts.

You can even introduce innovative pricing, for example, if the gyms charge payments for a monthly membership; you can offer a weekly membership or pay as you go scheme if the member wants to try for few days. This kind of innovative pricing can have a great boost in customers because the customers are not required to purchase the membership for one full month. This kind of setup gives them an opportunity to try the gym for a few days and if they are satisfied they can convert for monthly or yearly memberships. This will also attract the traveling crowd that is visiting the city for a few days. The biggest advantage of this is that the gym will be able to build a huge database of customers to contact for their future offerings.

Another innovative marketing strategy that you can adopt is to visit general practitioners in the area and ask for a recommendation from them. A doctor can recommend a patient who requires weight loss, or a diabetic patient in need of regular exercises to the gym. A recommendation coming from a respected doctor can boost the image of the gym in the area. This can even result in the development of products that are aimed for specific markets like diabetes or weight loss.

New year resolutions are the best way to target prospective customers because people often resolve to pay attention to their fitness in the new year but are unable to stick to their goals. A gym can install tracking software for such resolutions and send the reminder messages to motivate them to attend regular gym sessions. This will have a positive impact on the mind of the customer who will gladly spread of word about the gym.

The gym can even host the weight loss program for the community and encourage the users to post the updates on their social media page. Social media has got a huge reach and if done correctly this kind of programs can become viral and attract the attention of people rapidly. A gym can also declare a cash reward or free membership to the winner of such challenge and the participants of the challenge can be offered a special discount in gym memberships.

The gym can even host the featured member scheme. People who attend the gym sessions regularly to achieve their fitness goals must be rewarded by featuring them in gym campaigns and social media page. This will also send a message to the prospective members that the gym cares and supports people to achieve their fitness goals. The featured members could be rewarded with a free t-shirt or a gym bag as a token of appreciation for their hard work.

The gym can also offer refrigerator magnets to their members for free or the gym can distribute free branded pens. Usually, the magnets and pens are very cheap and do not cost much, and they provide use boost to the brand of the gym. This is a very important part of a brand promotion that is often ignored.

You can check every follower that the gym has on Instagram, chances are that these followers could have a large following of people that makes them micro influencers for the gym. Usually, these micro influencers have more than 1000 followers. These people could be offered special discounts or additional facilities at the gym for sharing the pictures and videos of their workouts on their Instagram profile. The message instantly reaches to their followers and these followers could be offered a special discount along with a free trial membership.

It could be that some people have never heard about your gym, you can even search the influencers by the hashtags, for example, if your gym provides facilities for a traditional workout then you can search for the hashtag #traditionalworkout. This way it becomes very easy to reach potential influencers who might be interested in partnering with the gym to promote its services.

The gym can even invite journalists from the local newspapers or influential bloggers in the area for free sessions at the gym. They could be encouraged to explore various facilities offered by the gym and if they are satisfied and happy then they will surely put a word on their blog or write up in a newspaper. These kinds of strategies can boost the image of the gym in the eyes of prospective customers.

Direct mail can also be influential in attracting new customers, it is a fact that people love to sift through the direct mails and a personalized gym postcard result in sales of new memberships. The act of sending regular postcards at regular intervals can also help in better brand retention for the customer. Even if the customer does not buy the membership immediately he will still recall the brand in a positive way as soon as he sees it on the internet.

The gym can offer a special incentive to every visitor on its website. This will usually increase the amount of prospective customers visiting the gym. If the gym is offering a free session then it could offer the customer an opportunity to schedule his visit online. Today's tech-savvy customers love to schedule their bookings online. In this way, the gym will be able to keep track of the number of prospective customers visiting the gym. This could also provide a huge boost in the sales of membership of the gym.

The gym can also offer special discounts to the customers signing up through social media websites like Facebook or Instagram. These websites have the potential to reach a large number of targeted customers in the shortest possible time. The regular sharing of pictures and videos on the social media websites can increase customer engagement because people love to share pictures and videos. The gym can prepare a video showing the customer having fun while performing the exercises; it could even show how personal trainers take care of the customers. This kind of videos can generate a positive sentiment in the mind of a prospective customer and could result in higher memberships.

The gym can also undertake various activities like weekly get together or a monthly hiking program so that the users can engage with each other and remain motivated to attend the gym for regular sessions. These kinds of efforts delight the customer and make him feel special.

The marketing strategy should be geared towards the increased satisfaction of the customer. Whatever a gym does it must be focused solely on the customer.

The beauty of Facebook is that it allows the advertisers to laser target their customers. The targeting power is such that it allows targeting a single stay-at-home dad, who also happens to love a dog and listen to the radio as a recreational activity. Facebook can reach almost any market that you can imagine, and gives you, the marketer, the power to put your message in front of them.

However, Facebook requires a little bit of tweaking because it is different than another platform which enables you to sell directly to customers, the audience of Facebook is a bit different because most people use Facebook for connecting with their friends, share interesting posts, etc. That is why a Facebook user might not be in an immediate hurry to buy products because they are not searching for anything to buy. As a marketer, the audience of Facebook has to be nurtured. Facebook as an advertising platform provides higher returns on advertising spend compared to other networks. If you are lucky as a marketer if done right Facebook can generate an insane amount of sales with spending of a few hundred dollars.

There are a lot of people who have not been successful with Facebook when you try to convince your client to sell on Facebook, often you will hear that Facebook advertising didn't work for their business, this is normal because there are businesses who are doing the same thing. You have to be able to convince your client that people who do not see any results with Facebook advertising is because either they have very little knowledge to understand the elements that create successful campaigns or these people quit when they don't see any results. The most important reason is that people often end up hiring a wrong person to handle their marketing campaigns.

These problems can be avoided if the company hires the right individual as their marketing consultant. The service-based businesses require a different approach than the products based businesses. If the campaign is properly optimized it is possible to get best ROI. Here you can explain to your client that if his service commands a higher price premium then he will have ROI compared to the person whose service commands a lower price premium. You must also explain to your client he can expect to see the results soon.

Some people think advertising on Facebook is an easy task, but it demands hard work and willingness to learn, something that your client might possess due to the paucity of time. You have to get a clear budget from your client because if the budget is too low, the results might not be visible. Online advertising can consume the budgets very quickly, thus if you have an idea of money to spend beforehand, you could plan a campaign in such a way that it leaves very little scope for failure. You cannot just go ahead and start the campaign and sit back. You have to convince your client that you will be running a low budget campaign initially to see what type of campaign works. You can explain that if he spends all his at once, then he might be disappointed. You, as a marketing consultant are concerned for his success and thus would like to take baby steps. This will help build the trust between you and the client.

Working with independent contractors

You will be working with a freelancer or independent contractors for the project. However, there are legal requirements that must be satisfied to avoid any legal hassles later on. A graphic designer can be defined as an independent contractor because you are paying him for utilizing his services and he is not your regular employee. The misclassification between an employee and an independent contractor can result in heavy penalties later on.

Each payment that is made to the independent contractor should be well documented, a person must sign form W-9 before starting the work, you have to check his taxpayer identification number and if he does not have the taxpayer identification number then you are required to withhold the tax payment.

It is also important to get proper documents like resume or qualification documents and verify them. It must be made clear in the contract that the invitation to work is not as an employee of the company but as an independent contractor. It would also be prudent to collect references of previous projects completed by the freelancer and ask for any documentary evidence like license or incorporation agreement that establishes his status as an independent contractor.

A written contract is very necessary because it specifies the terms of the employment. The contract must explicitly state that the freelancer is being employed on the project as an independent contractor and must be signed by both parties; you must also define the nature of the work and the expected deadlines when the work would be completed. The payment schedule must be drawn up indicating how payments will be made and the penalty if either party violates the contract. The contract must also mention the ownership of the work done by the freelancer in the project; make sure to put everything in writing to avoid legal troubles later on.

You can also sign on a non-compete agreement with the freelancer. Often a freelancer works in a project, after the expiry of the project he directly approaches the client and hampers the relationship between the client and the consultant. A Non-compete agreement would forbid the freelancer from performing such act.

If you plan to pay more than $600 to a freelancer in a year then you will have to report these details in form 1099-MISC and give the copy of this to the freelancer working for you.

More Books In The Series

STEP BY STEP GUIDE TO SURVIVE AS COPYWRITER

STEP BY STEP GUIDE TO PET SITTING BUSINESS

STEP BY STEP GUIDE TO DIGITAL MARKETING CONSULTING BUSINESS

STEP BY STEP GUIDE TO DENTAL CLINIC MARKETING CONSULTING BUSINESS

STEP BY STEP GUIDE TO RESAURANT MARKETING CONSULTING BUSINESS

STEP BY STEP GUIDE TO YOGA CENTER CONSULTING BUSINESS

STEP BY STEP GUIDE TO AEROBIC CENTER CONSULTING BUSINESS

www.ingramcontent.com/pod-product-compliance
Lightning Source LLC
Chambersburg PA
CBHW031525210526
45464CB00007B/3024